TOWARDS
A PEOPLE'S
CONSTITUTION FOR
BOTSWANA

FOREWORD BY YASH GHAI, EMERITUS PROFESSOR OF LAW UNIVERSITY OF HONG KONG; CHAIR OF CONSTITUTION OF KENYA REVIEW COMMISSION 2001-4

I0479745

OAGILE BETHUEL KEY DINGAKE

INDIA · SINGAPORE · MALAYSIA

Notion Press

No.8, 3rd Cross Street,
CIT Colony, Mylapore,
Chennai, Tamil Nadu – 600004

First Published by Notion Press 2020
Copyright © Oagile Bethuel Key Dingake 2020
All Rights Reserved.

ISBN 978-1-64951-631-2

CONTENTS

FOREWORD

In Africa for long time the making of a constitution normally followed the end of the colonial regime. The colonial authority had considerable influence on the making of the new constitution, requiring, as the price for independence, that it provide for democracy as well as other rights of the people. A second phase of constitution making was, rather, constitution unmaking as the new politician leaders shifted to authoritarianism.

The experience of Botswana was however different. First its decolonization constitution was based on the traditional system in which chiefs played the key role. Second, that constitution has remained in effect, though not without some amendment. Botswana has never had a coup. It is a great compliment to the leaders under that constitution that in all that period, Botswana has flourished as an independent, peaceful state.

In this excellent contribution to what he tells us is a debate already under way, Justice Dingake while acknowledging the critical role of the current constitution, since its establishment in 1966 on independence, proposes its replacement by a very different form. He does this because the Botswana of the present day is very different from when it achieved its independence from the British.

Justice Dingake, now a judge, also a former teacher and scholar, has proposed, in his scholarly way, a transformative constitution. No doubt that it would attract great interest among not only the people of Botswana, but also throughout Africa and other places—among politicians, governments and scholars. Not derogating from the existing system or those who run it, he has put his case so convincingly—and tactfully-- that few would quarrel with his proposals. Now this itself is a major achievement in all of Africa—and elsewhere. However, somehow one has the feeling that among many politicians in Africa -- who tend to resist any limits on their powers -- there would be great resistance to the proposals.

As an African scholar who has played some role in the making of a few constitutions in African (and other) states, I am very impressed by the way Justice Dingake presents his argument. He makes an excellent case for the transfer to a new system. He puts in an excellent and convincing way how Botswana should move to a new constitution. He has established an excellent case for the changes he has proposed. It is unnecessary to say that he has a masterly understanding of the African experience with past and present constitutions—and frequently draws on them, focusing on those relatively successful in constitutional transitions.

In Justice Dingake's scheme the victory would be of the people. His emphasis is on the mode of constitution making, He pays close attention to the role of the ordinary citizens or groups in the making of the constitution— in initiating it, developing the agenda, elaborating its contents and importance. Apart from that, he points to the importance of citizens in the implementation of the Constitution. He favours people driven constitutions— and points to the role that people have played in some countries, particularly Kenya.

The purpose of his book is to provide guidance for the drafting (and acceptance) of the new constitution for his country. It provides ample guidance. He traces very well the imperative of human rights (of which he is a profound and ardent scholar). I like in particular his references to the Charter of the African Union, and the African Charter on Human and People's Rights to which, alas, sufficient attention is not generally given. He reminds us that the values of the Union Charter are "freedom, equality, justice, peace and human dignity". It is critical that these values become law automatically for Union member states. He says a constitution is more than legal rules: "it is a visionary document, expresses the aspirations of the people, securing the future".

Perhaps his notion of a constitution is over-optimistic: "A Constitution is the glue that keeps the nation together, irrespective of the social standing of its people, religious beliefs and political differences". However, it is necessary to be a little cautious about the role of the people. Kenya is both a good and a bad example. While in the first part of the process of constitution making, the people's wishes dominated those of politicians, soon the politicians took over despite their small numbers.

It must be said that popular participation in implementation of the Kenyan constitution has met resistance from politicians, and has been less effective than reading the document would suggest. The question is for how long civil society can dominate politics, especially when its ability to work together is somewhat limited.

YASH GHAI, *Emeritus Professor of Law University of Hong Kong; Chair of Constitution of Kenya Review Commission 2001-4; Founder/Director of Katiba Institute, Nairobi.*

PREFACE

Botswana is on the verge of a constitutional review process. This is so because all major parties have publicly committed to initiating a constitutional review process. The current constitution was adopted in 1966 and has not been fundamentally revised since then. The new consensus on constitutional review is long overdue as Botswana has been overtaken by countries that obtained independence much later than she did in terms of crafting constitutions whose bill of rights are much more inclusive and also in terms of entrenching institutions that support democracy.

The purpose of this booklet is to share my thoughts on the process and the possible content of the constitution to be crafted. The main target is the general public, political parties, civil society and other stakeholders who may want the constitution revised to entrench democracy and the rule of law.

In the last two decades, constitutional making across the globe has assumed greater importance in the quest for democracy, constitutionalism, good governance and the rule of law. In Africa, Kenya, Malawi, Tanzania, Zambia and Zimbabwe have in the last decade or so embarked on constitutional review processes that yielded mixed results.

At the end of the day there is no uniform method of constitution making in the world, but there are certain principles that modern constitution making should fulfil in order to have a constitution that people may feel they own and represents their interests. This includes a transparent and people-driven process that is properly planned and budgeted for. Additionally, care must be taken that political parties and the elites do not hijack the process from the people. It is also important that civil society must be empowered to meaningfully participate in the constitution making process. There is indeed evidence, in some parts of Africa, that civil society has been able to articulate, the aspirations, concerns and fears of the people better than political parties.

This booklet also reflects on the constitution making processes of some countries in Africa such as South Africa, Namibia, Malawi, Tanzania, Kenya, Zambia and Zimbabwe in the context of the involvement of the people. The reflection takes into account that as a general rule a constitution of any country is a product of the circumstances and history of that particular country. It follows therefore that the constitutional review process and the end product must reflect Botswana's own history and circumstances. Botswana can consciously avoid the errors that some of the above countries made that ended up in a constitution whose legitimacy was still open to credible criticism.

CHAPTER ONE

INTRODUCTION

Botswana is on the verge of a constitutional review process. The purpose of this publication is to share my thoughts on the process and principles that a constitutional review exercise should follow and the possible substantive constitutional provisions the nation may wish to adopt or debate in the event such an exercise eventually takes place, as seems likely.

The target audience is the general public and other key stakeholders who have a keen interest in the constitution making process. In order to promote readership of as many people as possible I attempt to write in simple language free of unnecessary jargon. This is clearly not an academic piece; and is deliberately uncluttered with references.

Consequently, my discussion of both the process and possible content of constitutional provisions is general in nature, and is meant to trigger a debate on the kind of constitution, the nation wants for the future. None of the thoughts expressed in this publication are intended to be prescriptive. It is hoped the publication would induce some further reflections by politicians who may not have reflected much on the kind of constitution they want the country to have in the future. If in the process of reading this book the people or the political parties are able to pick one or two ideas that can have a meaningful impact on the lives of the people, especially ordinary people, then the publication would have achieved its purpose.

I state from the onset that a constitution making process should be participatory and people driven. This emanates from the democratic right of the people as the repository of sovereign power to make a constitution they desire. It is important that the end result of a constitutional review process must reflect the views of all Batswana, as to what they want reflected in a new constitution. It is not suggested that any proposed views herein are necessarily the desirable ones. The desirable ones will come from the people after they have reflected on their collective challenges and wishes.

For a very long time the issue of a possible constitutional review was found in academic circles, pockets of civil society and the political opposition. In recent years, a sundry cacophony of voices calling for constitutional review grew louder. It is a positive development that, for the first in many years, all major political parties have reached a consensus and consider that the process of constitutional review should now be undertaken. This is a significant juncture in the history of our republic.

It is important that we review our constitution with the aim of crafting a uniquely Botswana constitution; that builds on our journey in nurturing and entrenching a democratic republic that subscribes to the rule of law.

Botswana have the opportunity to craft a constitution of their dreams, being careful not to be too idealistic, but as practical as the circumstances and reality of our republic demands. We have the opportunity to craft a constitution in accord with our broad socio-economic and political reality and circumstances; an implementable blue print that can serve our nation better for many decades to come.

More significantly, we have an opportunity to craft a constitution that can entrench a limited and accountable government that has functioning institutions of democracy, and embraces all human rights as prescribed in international legal instruments. A constitution that does not tolerate the so called "big man syndrome" or one-man rule that has plagued Africa for too long, is what the country needs. Our constitution must reflect the truth that any person entrusted with power is susceptible to abusing it and that it is imperative the law should constrain and regulate the exercise of power.

The pending constitutional review process may benefit from a functioning all party conference where political parties can debate matters of national and mutual interest, and reach common ground, with a view to properly guide the nation. This platform, which is not there in many countries, may smoothen the constitutional making process.

It is also hoped that all the major political players yearn for a genuine, open process that is not elite-centred and controlled; and that none of the players would seek to highjack the process in any manner and form so that the process becomes a mere sham or fails to advance the interests of the people. Whilst this is always a risk in any politically contested terrain, it is hoped that the people shall remain united to ensure the process is open, genuine and does not serve narrow political interests.

An openness of the process ensures that the people develop a real sense that they indeed own the constitution, and that the constitution is not owned by certain individuals or interest groups. This is consistent with the African Union vision as found in many of its documents. The Charter of the African union highlights the imperative to realize values of freedom, equality, justice, peace and human dignity. The above aspirations have recently been reinforced through the adoption of the African Union Agenda 2063: *The Africa We Want*, more relevantly, through aspiration three (3) which aspires for an Africa in which human rights and the rule of law are respected.

The idea of a constitutional review is borne by our own experience with running a democratic state. In the course of the last 53 years or so, our people have noticed some gaps and possible areas of development. They have often expressed a wish to close any perceived loopholes in their constitution, and building a more resilient democratic system that is consistent with the national democratic vision of a prosperous and democratic society. The courts have tried their best to develop the constitution, but there is a limit to what the courts can do without being accused of trespassing into the sphere of legislation.

It is correct to say that our constitution, notwithstanding some inadequacies, has served us well, in that although we had fundamental differences on some aspects, such as an inadequate bill of rights, unequal constitutional recognition of the various nationalities that constitute the Botswana nation, refusal or reluctance to recognize fully the rights of the San, powers of the president, lack of independence of watchdog institutions, such as the Directorate on Corruption and Economic Crime (DCEC), we still managed to live together in harmony and peace and used the courts to address our grievances. Economically, we have made advances that have earned us the admiration of the world although unemployment, inequality and poverty remains endemic.

With the benefit of hindsight, it is perhaps fair to opine that the nationalist leaders who negotiated our constitution may have thought it more urgent to achieve self–rule; than to embark on a long drawn out democratic exercise that would have allowed the people to participate in the crafting of their constitution. Practical considerations such as high levels of illiteracy then, and difficulties of an effective outreach program may have been considered a disadvantage. The situation is now different. Contemporary Botswana ranks amongst the highest in terms of literacy rates in Africa, in addition, roads networks and other avenues of reaching people have increased phenomenally since independence.

The inadequacy of our post-independence order has been criticized mildly by many scholars, but more robustly by Kgosi Kgafela who called for a home-grown constitution. He even wrote me a letter asking that I volunteer myself as an expert witness in a case he intended to file to declare the constitution illegitimate. He did indeed bring such a case before court and somehow it never saw the light of the day. His efforts fell in the genre of litigation that constitutional scholars call transformative litigation.

In my mind we missed the opportunity to have the court pronounce itself on the most intractable constitutional litigation of our time. The contention that the constitution must be declared illegitimate is a rarity in constitutional litigation. I do believe Kgosi Kgafela deserves more credit than we have hitherto been prepared to give him, as a nation, in the area of constitutional development.

Since independence, thanks to general prudent management of the country and respect of the rule of law, the country achieved enduring peace, stability and social cohesion. Now, having achieved stability, peace and a democratic system, although not without flaws, the time has arisen, to craft a new constitution that would capture our aspirations as a nation, recognizing, as we should, the inherent dignity and the equal and inalienable rights of all people, as recognized in all major international human rights instruments, as a foundation for freedom, justice, liberty, peace and unity.

In crafting a better constitutional dispensation than the one we currently have, we must of necessity not seek to reinvent the wheel, but we should be willing to learn from the other nations, especially those in Africa, and attempt to avoid the pitfalls or shortcomings of their processes. At the end of the day however, the constitution must be a product of our history and circumstances. It should not be a fashionable and fanciful document that does not resonate with the unique circumstances of the country.

When it comes to nations, a constitution is the social contract. It details how people are to coexist as a polity, and how they are to be governed. A constitution contains the rules of how a country is to be run, hence the statement that it is a social contract. But in a developing democracy, a constitution is more than a set of legal rules and norms; it is a visionary document, expressing the aspirations of the people. It secures the future, by ensuring a design that is purpose-made for progress, development and growth.

All developing nations are of necessity transitional societies that are moving from an undesirable past, often of poor governance and human rights violations or constitutions that were not designed to promote democracy; by building supporting institutions and constraining the exercise of arbitrary power by those who may be in charge at any given time. We need a constitution that can assist in tackling underdevelopment and usher a future in which development and prosperity of every individual is possible.

We need a constitution that would discourage the abuse of power. A constitution of necessity must mistrust those in power and seek to restrain and make them accountable to the people. It must have been the French philosopher Montesquieu who wrote, in a timeless remark, that:

> *"Political liberty is to be found only where there is no abuse of power. But constant experience shows that every man invested with power is liable to abuse it and carry his authority as far as it would go… To prevent this abuse, it is necessary from the nature of things that one power should be a check on another… When the legislative and executive powers are united in the same person or body, there can be no liberty… Again there is no liberty if the judicial power is not separated from the legislative and executive… There would be an end of everything if the same person or body whether of the nobles or of the people, were to exercise all three powers."*

Conceptually, a constitution is the mother of all laws. It has amongst its essential functions, the distribution of power among the various organs of the state. The manner of distribution of power is a function of the country's history and the future aspirations of the nation. A constitution is the glue that keeps the nation together, irrespective of the social standing of its people, religious beliefs and political affiliations.

A constitution should respect and protect the rights of every person. It is for this reason that the constitution is often referred to as the "mirror" or "soul" of the nation. It is useful to see the constitution as a full body mirror. It must reflect everyone without exception, including the poor and the marginalized. If it reflects only the image of the privileged, then it is a constitution of only those people and not all the people.

In a country where the constitution is supreme, no legislative act contrary to the constitution can be valid. A constitution can never be perfect, but it must come to as close as possible to perfection. There is no constitution that is perfect in the world. Even the constitutions considered amongst the best in the world have flaws, and there is always an ongoing effort to develop and improve them. In that sense, a constitution is better treated as 'work- in progress'.

A constitution codifies the principles of constitutionalism, among them the rule of law, equality, separation of powers, judicial independence, collaborative governance and universal adult suffrage. But a constitution provides an opportunity for more. It provides the opportunity to design mechanisms to achieve good governance, management of public resources, and of establishing a society of justice, accountability, transparency, and the protection of individual human rights and freedoms.

CHAPTER TWO

BACKGROUND CONTEXT

In the introductory chapter much emphasis was made about the need for the constitution to take into account the country's history and circumstances. This chapter therefore sets the scene, for the subsequent chapters, by discussing, briefly, how Botswana gained nationhood and the idea of a constitution in broad terms, in the context of historic influences of democratic constitutions, the world over, such as the Magna Carta. The Magna Carta outlined fundamental rights and freedoms that are today reflected in one form or another in national constitutions of many countries.

Nationhood

Botswana gained independence from Britain in 1966. The constitution was a colonial imposition and the people played no part in its formulation. It provided the legal framework by which the new nation was formed. With the adoption of the constitution, Botswana became a republic and the old way of governance, in which various tribes/communities were ruled by chiefs was discarded in favour of a centralized unitary state ruled by an elected political leadership. The constitution retained an advisory role for the chiefs, in the form of what today is called *Ntlo ya Dikgosi,* (House of Chiefs)

The constitution defines the identity of the people and territory that comprise the nation-state, establishes a system of government to govern the collective affairs of the people and declares and guarantees protection of the rights of its people and other persons. For instance, the bill of rights recognizes the rights of "every person" not necessarily citizens only.

It is often correctly said that the constitution is the soul of the nation. It is organic and futuristic in nature, designed not only to serve the needs of the current generation, but generations yet unborn. It is also elastic and designed to protect all its people, at all times, not just a particular section of the populace. The constitution demands total respect and obedience from its people, including the leadership of the country.

Modern constitutions are written in simple language so that they may be read, internalized and understood by everyone. The Botswana constitution could do with further simplification of the language employed. This would improve accessibility and the sense of ownership amongst its people. It is also important that it must be written in all languages spoken in Botswana.

Supremacy of the Constitution

Although the constitution of Botswana does not expressly provide that it is the supreme law of the land; it has been interpreted to be so. Being the supreme law of the land means that all other laws are subject to it. Statutes and subordinate enactments and actions taken under them are read subject to the constitution and any such acts that are inconsistent with the constitution are, to the extent of their inconsistency, invalid. In interpreting the constitution, the judges must give effect to what it commands and its values. They should not place themselves above the constitution.

Parliament is the supreme law-making body. It is bound to pass laws for the good governance and order of the country. Such laws should not conflict with the constitution. The executive is responsible for policy formulation. The Court of Appeal, which is the apex court, is the final arbiter of constitutional issues. All arms of government are responsible to, answerable and accountable to the constitution for their actions.

The High Court and the Court of Appeal have the authority to strike out as unconstitutional any law or policy that is inconsistent with the constitution. Since independence, many statutes enacted by the legislature have been struck down by the High Court and the Court of Appeal, as unconstitutional. The recent example, in June 2019, is the decision of the High Court declaring section 164 of the Penal Code, which penalized gay sex, unconstitutional. They have been many other similar instances before.

Although the constitution is amenable to alteration, it should not be amended too frequently. It is in the nature of a constitution that it must be an enduring document. However, the constitution may be altered when it is absolutely necessary from time to time to keep pace with changing conditions over time. The constitution contains provisions for alterations to be made under stringent procedures designed to ensure that adequate time is given to the members of parliament and the public to comment on the proposed change and adequate opportunity is given for meaningful debate in parliament. Changes to ordinary provisions of the constitution require a simple majority, whilst entrenched provisions require at least two thirds majority.

Law-makers should be slow to alter the basic structure of the constitution unless the proposed amendment has the required support of the population. What exactly is the basic structure of the constitution may be subject to debate. However, it is generally acknowledged that basic structure is something sacred and fundamental to the governance of the country, such as being a secular democratic republic, separation of powers, and certain fundamental rights like the right to equality and fundamental freedoms. The courts often guard against undue and unjustifiable alteration of the basic structure of the constitution.

Separation of Powers

The demarcation of powers between the three arms of government is implicit in the constitution. Reading the constitution as a whole there is no doubt that the principle of separation of powers is imbedded in the structure of government established by the constitution. Provisions are designed to ensure that each arm of government operates within their respective sphere of influence.

The constitution also provides interlinkages, checks and balances between the three arms of government to ensure that they function effectively as a government. For this reason, the interactions between the three arms of government inevitably overlap at different points. As a result, the divide between the three arms of government is sometimes blurred. However, in the event of any serious ambiguity the superior courts have the final authority to clarify the boundaries of each sphere of influence.

Concerns around the precise boundaries of the three organs of the state, namely, the legislature, the executive and the judiciary are not unique to Botswana. Similar debates have occurred in many parliamentary democracies including the United Kingdom, Australia, Kenya, Zambia and South Africa. The Court of Appeal in Botswana has made it clear that separation of powers in Botswana is loose. For instance, members of parliament may also be members of the executive.

Limits to Government Power and Protected Rights

The limits on legislative and executive power in favour of protected civil and political rights of the people is reflected in the constitution. The Botswana constitution only entrenches civil and political rights. A law or proposed law that seeks to regulate or restrict a fundamental right or qualified right must be authorised by the constitution. Such a law must be reasonably justifiable in a democratic society. This test is not regarded as sufficiently high to protect human rights. Constitutions that provide a higher test provide that any limitation of rights must be shown to be necessary in a democratic society. Case law from a number of jurisdictions has held that the "necessary" test is higher than "reasonably justifiable in a democratic society".

Judicial Independence

The constitution does not precisely provide for the independence of the judiciary, although it is clear from an examination of the constitution as a whole that the judiciary was intended by the framers of the constitution to be independent. The judiciary exercises judicial power delegated to it by the people. In fact all power by the organs of the state belongs to the people. The legislative power rests with parliament acting through their duly elected representatives. Modern constitutions do not leave the matter of the independence of the judiciary to guess work. They expressly say that the judiciary shall be independent of anyone.

Judicial authority is exclusively exercised by the courts that are independent of the other arms of the state. The Judiciary is regarded as the custodian of the constitution and the laws of Botswana. It is the courts that interpret and apply the laws and in the process ensure that the laws are adhered to. An independent, effective and efficient court system that dispenses justice in a fair, timely and efficient manner is one of the important preconditions for maintaining the rule of law and sustaining a peaceful society. Judicial independence is an indispensable element of a democratic society. It holds the key to maintenance of the law, to sustaining democratic rule and holding together the fabric of the democratic society.

The Botswana judiciary is amongst the most independent of judiciaries of modern democracies. Many of the tenets of judicial independence that we find in our constitution which we take for granted are envied by many developing countries and some developed democracies. For instance, one can hardly remember a single case in which any of the arms of government willfully failed to obey an order of court as is common in many jurisdictions. The individual and collective independence of judges in judicial decision-making is zealously guarded against external and internal interference or influence. The only legitimate criticism with respect to the independence of the judiciary is that the law does not give the judiciary adequate autonomy to manage its own finances.

Most constitutions of the world, including Botswana have been influenced in some way by the Magna Carta.

The Magna Carta, often referred to as the Great Charter of English liberties was formulated in 1215 and reissued with alterations in 1216, 1217 and 1225. It outlined liberties held by "free men" and declared the sovereign to be subject to the rule of law. When William the Conqueror invaded Britain around the 11th century, the British Barons lost many of the privileges which they had previously enjoyed and many of their lands and forests were taken for the exclusive use of the King and his followers. This included lands and other property of the Church.

William ruled in an arbitrary and oppressive manner. He set aside the laws made by Edward the Confessor, also known as Saint Edward the Confessor, and gave the property he had taken from the English people to reward followers and taking it back if it pleased him. Kings William I, William Rufus, Henry I and Stephen were all petitioned by the Barons to reinstate the rights enjoyed under King Edward. Many promises were made by the Kings when their power was weak and they needed support, but few kept those promises. On or around 1100, Henry I issued a charter of liberties declaring that the Church shall be free, that heirs shall receive their possession unredeemed, and that evil customs shall be abolished, but no other steps were taken to reinstate the "common law" of Edward.

Around 1199 John ascended to the throne. He was not the direct heir of King Richard, whose son Arthur should have been the heir to the Crown of England. But

John and his friends campaigned with the Barons for his elevation promising a confirmation of Henry I's Charter and a renewal of the Anglo-Saxons laws instituted by Edward the Conqueror. Having ascended to the throne with the Barons' assistance gave the Barons hope that these promise would actually be kept by King John.

John was crowned by consent of the Barons on 27 May, 1199 but maintained the tradition of his forebears, and hardly kept any of his promises or that of his forebears. The frustration of the Barons grew and they commenced a series of meetings with the Bishops of the Church with whom they made common cause. These meetings resulted in a number of petitions being made to the King resulting in more promises but no action. Eventually King John conceded to all of the demands, and the Magna Carta was signed and sealed on 15 June 1215.

While the Magna Carta can correctly be regarded as a foundation of democracy in Great Britain, the truth is that it was concerned solely with controlling the arbitrary exercise of royal power interfering with the rights, privileges and property of the Barons, the Knights and other freemen. It was not concerned with the rights of the common man. As indicated earlier, subsequent Kings reissued the Charter. In 1225 Henry III gave, in his third confirmation, the final form to Magna Carta. The common law received in Magna Carta its first generally recognised statute, written law, authoritative at the date of its publication. Around 1297, Edward I and parliament, in putting Magna Carta on the statute rolls, effectively imposed Magna Carta on the courts "as common law". At the time the Magna Carta was a very progressive document that included articles that provided that:

> *XXXVIII No Bailiff, for the future, shall put any man to his law, upon his own simple affirmation, without credible witnesses produced for that purpose.*

> *XXXIX No free man shall be seized, or imprisoned or dispossessed or outlawed, or in any way destroyed; nor will we condemn him, nor will we commit him to prison, except by the legal judgment of his peers, or by the laws of the land.*

With the passage of time, particularly commencing around the 15th century to the 17th century Magna Carta was largely ignored by parliament and the courts but enjoyed a revival during the reigns of James I and Charles I against what was perceived to be a growing tyranny in State and Church and a parliament dominated by members enjoying the distribution to them of church lands.

The Magna Carta, more well- known articles included the following:

- The services of free men not to be demanded, with some exceptions in the interests of the Sate.

- That courts would operate separately from the Court of the King and that they would sit at fixed places at fixed times.

- Priority be given to Crown debts in the administration of deceased estates.

- Penalties be proportionate to the crime.

- Crown officers not to take goods or services except for payment or by consent.

- Imposing on the King a duty to remove those who come with arms to enter the kingdom with intent to damage it.

- Any interference by the Pope to be considered null and void.

- A tribunal of 25 Barons was set up to deal with any alleged failure to abide by the Charter.

Magna Carta did not protect England from civil war as the war of 1642-1648 resulted in the King being dethroned and decapitated and a republic set up under Oliver Cromwell. However, over the next two centuries from 1688 parliament became an indispensable source of governmental functions with ministerial responsibility to parliament and parliamentary sovereignty over the sovereign King.

Magna Carta ceased to have any meaningful influence in England but its influence in the new colonies in America was phenomenal. It was invoked in court and treated as fundamental law and many of its concepts embodied in the constitutions of the United States particularly Virginia and Massachusetts. Legislators imported copies from England and William Penn published at Philadelphia an edition of Magna Carta and other constitutional documents from England.

Many of the provisions of the US Constitution of 1789 such as those dealing with: ex post facto laws, laws on the law of contracts, taxation by the legislature only, habeas corpus, trial by jury in criminal cases, laws imposing religious tests, came from Magna Carta or other contemporary English constitutional documents. But the 1789 constitution did not contain a bill of rights concerning the liberties of individual citizens. Subsequent amendments were inspired by the Magna Carta. For instance, the Fifth Amendment inter-alia, provided that "no person shall be deprived of life, liberty, or property without the due process of law; nor shall private property be taken for public use without just compensation".

The 14th Amendment, similarly inspired by the Magna Carta, provided, inter-alia, that "no State shall make or enforce any law which shall abridge the privileges or immunities of citizens of the United States; nor shall any State deprive any person of life, liberty, or property without due process of law; nor deny to any person within its jurisdiction the equal protection of the laws."

An Overview of Early Constitutions

The United States constitution is one of the first modern written national constitutions which has influenced the formation of constitutions around the world. The European Convention of Human Rights of 1952/3 has also had a similar effect, especially on former

British colonies. Such influence is also palpable in the constitutions of Netherlands and Norway which became constitutional democracies in 1814, Belgium in 1831, Denmark in 1849, Argentina in 1853, Luxembourg in 1868, and Australia in 1901.

The United States constitution which is quite concise, is one of the shortest and India one of the longest. The brief nature of the US constitution means it contained a lot of ambiguities that required constant clarification. This has led to the supreme court having to interpret some of the ambiguities which arise from time to time and to make it adaptable to changing historic circumstances and ensure it remains relevant in times far removed from the one in which it was written.

Definition

A popular definition of a constitution is that it is a set of fundamental principles according to which a state is governed. It essentially establishes the state and distributes power amongst the various organs that make up the state. Some constitutions, such as the constitution of the United Kingdom, are not codified, but written in numerous fundamental Acts of the legislature, court cases or treaties. As it is often said, to the surprise of many, the United Kingdom has an unwritten constitution.

Constitutions fall under two broad groups: the "presidential" and the "parliamentary" systems.

The fundamental difference is usually the method of selecting and removing the head of government. In a presidential system, the president is mostly popularly elected, either directly or by means of an Electoral College system, such as in the United States. By contrast, the head of government in a parliamentary system, most often called the prime minister or premier, is selected by parliament.

In the presidential system, presidents are elected directly by the people. An example is the United States of America. In a presidential system it is fairly difficult to remove the president. By contrast in the parliamentary system the prime minister and his ministers continue in office by having a majority of the vote in parliament. The executive government can be removed by a no-confidence vote.

In a presidential system such as, for example, the United States, the president has to be impeached by charges brought against him and the lower house votes to impeach the president and the upper house has the authority to try the president of crimes against the State.

In a presidential system the president and his executive government have to persuade the representatives of the people of the desirability of the legislative programme. Even when the president is from the party which may have a majority in both houses, there is no guarantee that legislation will pass without amendment because members of the houses are mindful of their particular regional or constituency interests.

In contrast, in a parliamentary system where the prime minister's party has a strong majority in parliament the prime minister usually gets what he wants passed through parliament and differences are ironed out in cabinet before the bill is introduced. However, where the political situation of the country requires coalitions of parties to obtain a majority in either house, the same situation can apply as in the presidential system, because coalitions by nature require compromise.

In the presidential system, such as in the US, the president appoints the executive government. In the United Kingdom with a parliamentary system of government, the prime minister appoints the ministers of government and in both systems those appointees remain at the pleasure of the appointer.

It should be noted that the presidential and the parliamentary systems as explained above are not the only systems. There can be semi-presidential governments, where for example, the president appoints the prime minister and ministers but those appointees can only stay in power so long as they enjoy the support of parliament. France, has such an arrangement. For instance, in 1986-1988 the president of France lost a majority in the national assembly and was required to appoint his political opponent to the office of prime minister. Austria, Ireland, Iceland and Portugal have similar systems.

In Botswana which is a hybrid between the presidential and parliamentary systems, the president is bound to elect members of the executive from members of the national assembly. The president has the power to remove members of the executive without consulting parliament.

With the above background a consideration of the experiences of other countries in reviewing their constitutions may shed light on how best to approach the matter and what constitutional stipulations may be worth considering.

Constitutional Making/Reviews in Africa

South Africa and Namibia are often lauded for crafting progressive constitutions. However, it is important to state that much as we share a lot in common with South Africa and Namibia, their political circumstances before they adopted their democratic constitutions were in many material respects not similar to ours. Both countries were ruled by racist regimes that denied blacks any semblance of humanity. In fact, apartheid, that was the official policy in both countries, was declared a crime against humanity by the United Nations. We were lucky not to have come under the clutches of apartheid; and in fact established a functioning multi-party democratic state that opposed racism.

South Africa and Namibia are good examples of how constitution making can contribute to conflict resolution, and pave the way for a more democratic society. In South Africa the process of constitution making led to power-sharing that was necessary to achieve peace and stability. The 1993 interim constitution was a political pact, a power sharing agreement. The basic rationale for power sharing was to prevent forces of the past order threatening the new political order.

Compromises and concessions became inevitable because it was necessary to win over the old apartheid regime that still controlled the levers of power. This resulted in the government of national unity. The South African power sharing arrangement was to expire within five years and indeed it withered away and was replaced by a modified majority rule.

In Namibia, in 1981, all key stakeholders reached an agreement on the principles concerning the constituent assembly and the constitution of an independent Namibia. After its election in 1989, the constituent assembly unanimously adopted the principles as a framework for drawing up a constitution for the country. The Namibian approach to constitution making, although arguably not as comprehensive as in South Africa, in terms of consultation with the people, nevertheless ensured the participation of both the elites and the people in a manner that was generally satisfactory.

In South Africa, the 1993 interim constitution was the result of the work of the Multi-Party Negotiating Forum, which succeeded the Convention for a Democratic South Africa (CODESA) process, the latter also being a multi-party and multi-stakeholder forum. Subsequently, the 1996 final constitution was the result of a process led by the multi-party parliament, which doubled as a constitutional assembly.

The Groote Schuur Minute of May 1990 initiated in earnest the negotiation of the transition process from apartheid, at the centre of which was the adoption of a new constitution. The transition would be bi-staged; the first stage would feature the adoption of an interim constitution which provided for the election of a constitutional assembly, and a set of 34 constitutional principles would be a solemn pact to inform and shape the constitution-making process. The second stage would feature elections of a fully representative parliament which doubled up as constitutional assembly and the adoption of the new final constitution.

The interim constitution was born out of intense negotiations among key stakeholders. The interim constitution set out the principles governing the election of a constituent assembly through a proportional representation system. Before the election of the constituent assembly, while the interim constitution was in force, a government of national unity that was in power ensured that one group would not dominate the process of transition.

In Namibia, there was also a constitutional committee which scrutinized the draft constitution after it was submitted to the constituent assembly. In Namibia, services of experts were engaged. Expert contribution was not a substitute for people's participation. The people's participation was secured through evening lectures, seminars, discussions, and workshops were held to study a wide range of topics pertaining to constitutions, systems of government, the role of political parties in a multiparty democracy, and the international protection of human rights.

In South Africa, the expertise of the major players, on the main, obviated the need for sourcing experts externally. The importance of expertise cannot be over-emphasized. It contributes to effective and productive debates. The involvement of experts does not mean that they should dictate the content of the constitution. Their duty is to avail information to the people and explain concepts as may be necessary. Stakeholders meetings or conferences should not end up being sessions of experts.

The structure of the constitution making process is frequently an issue of contention among key participants. Some countries establish a constitutional review commission or a technical committee made up of representatives of key stakeholders, to oversee and coordinate the constitution review process. The above approach has been adopted recently by Zimbabwe, Zambia and Tanzania. Each country would invariably adopt an approach suitable to its own circumstances.

The process of revising old constitutions in Africa is slowly gathering pace. It is estimated that about 10 out of 54 African states have embarked on drafting new constitutions to reflect new thinking and aspirations in the recent past. In Southern and East Africa, Zimbabwe, Zambia, Tanzania and Kenya embarked on constitutional revisions.

In 2013, Zimbabwe adopted a new constitution, following a constitutional review process, that was often marred by controversy on, among other things, whether the consultative processes embarked upon were sufficiently inclusive or not. The constitution was one of the major achievements of an inclusive government that ruled Zimbabwe between 2009 and 2013.

A few years after the new constitution was adopted, debates still continue as to whether the new constitution was worth the effort, with many, although admitting some flaws in both the consultation process and the crafting of some substantive provisions, indicating that there was indeed an improvement to the preceding constitution. What seems to be of concern is that the new constitution is not being followed; and that subsidiary laws are not aligned to the constitution, leaving serious contradictions that have debilitating effect on good governance and the protection and promotion of human rights. There are also concerns that there are parts of the constitution that have never been implemented since its adoption in 2013. This includes Chapter 14 of the constitution on devolution.

Zimbabwe's road to constitutional reform was long. It featured, among other things, a failed referendum to adopt a new constitution in 2001. The multi-party parliament-led process was driven by the Constitutional Parliamentary Select Committee (COPAC) which was set up to spearhead the process, comprised of members of the three main parties in the unity government, and civil society representatives, co-chaired by nominated individuals from the parties in the unity government. Post 2001, the need for a new people-driven constitution became a key talking point in civil society and a point of contention between the government and the opposition.

In 2013, Zambia released a final draft of a new constitution that the technical committee had been working on since 2011. As at the time of writing this publication (2019) the process seems but all dead, following the rejection at a referendum of some innovative and progressive proposals to the bill of rights. The parties have also failed to reach agreement over modes of validating the draft document, and eventually adopting and enacting a final constitution. Generally, calls by civil society that government should establish clear and fair dialogue mechanisms have gone unheeded.

In Tanzania the process seems to have stalled. In 2010, President Jakaya Kikwete of Tanzania announced that there would be a constitutional review process, which should yield a new constitution in 2015. The whole process was seriously contested, with the opposition accusing the ruling party of having hijacked the process. The opposition charged further that the process had actually divided rather than united the country.

Several drafts of the constitution were made and the third and final draft of the constitution were released in September 2014. The process has not progressed any further. The referendum that was originally scheduled for April, 2015, never took place. There were concerns that the draft itself appeared to undermine the constitutional versions that emerged from public consultations.

In Kenya, the constitution-making process was a long road. After much reflection and pressure from civil society, with a very prominent role for women, a formal process of review began in 2001. It involved a constitutional commission and a national constitutional conference. The draft was then taken over by government, (quite contrary to the original design of the process). The resultant draft was rejected in a referendum in 2005. Following the post-election violence that broke out after the controversial December 2007 elections in which the renewed mandate of President Mwai Kibaki was alleged to be stolen, a team of mediators led by Kofi Annan, pushed for a renewed constitutional review process.

The national dialogue and reconciliation process led to an agreement between the parties in February 2008, including the formation of a government of national unity and other reforms. Agenda item 4 in the agreement focused on "Long-Term Issues", including constitutional and institutional reform.

In March 2008, the parties agreed on the principles for a constitutional review process, and parliament established a committee of experts on constitutional reform to gather views from the public, deliberate on contentious issues and come up with a draft of the new constitution, taking the earlier drafts as the starting point. The new body produced a draft, heavily based on the national constitutional conference version, then revised it in the light of public and expert comment. The revised draft then went to a parliamentary committee, which made some radical changes. The expert committee felt unable to resist the changes that touched on political power, including the change to a rather American-style presidential system rather than a parliamentary one. In August 2010, the draft constitution text was approved by a 67% margin in a national referendum

There are two practical lessons that come clearly out of the above discussion. The first one is that for a constitutional process to be legitimate, it must be genuinely people driven and not seek to advance the interests of the elites. Secondly, the process towards a new constitution is as important as crafting the substantive provisions of the constitution. It is absolutely important that "the people driven requirement" should not just be a mantra or a strategy designed to placate the people when the real aim is to impose on the people, a constitution that does not advance their interests but those of the elites.

It obviously cannot be disputed that constitution-making or reform is a pre-eminently political act that is always haunted by possibilities of betrayal.

Having regard to the above experiences it is important that Botswana must ensure that there is an inclusive participation of all political players, along with its citizens. A framework must be created to mitigate political contestation overshadowing national interest and the broad national vision of crafting its social contract.

CHAPTER THREE

THEORETICAL PERSPECTIVE ON CONSTITUTION – MAKING

In the decades past, emphasis in constitutional studies was in the main focused on the final contents or provisions of constitutions with limited regard to the importance of processes. This view has now changed and it is considered by many that the process is as important as the substantive provisions of the constitution. This is so because people's participation determine whether or not a constitution is legitimate.

A number of studies on constitution making have confirmed that the starting point is of necessity a political decision and the process is usually aimed at addressing a number of social, economic and political challenges. It follows therefore that a constitutional process must empower the people rather than inhibit them, by creating platforms and avenues for individual involvement.

At the end of the day the people must feel that the constitution that they have approved would improve good governance and contribute to solving the political, economic and social problems that they face, bearing in mind that no constitution can directly solve any socio-economic and political problems, but can certainly facilitate development.

Notwithstanding that public participation is increasingly recognized as imperative, the notion of public participation, in constitutional literature, has not been fully defined. However, it is a concept that is widely recognized by both international and regional legal instruments.

The right to participate in the affairs of one's nation is derived from the right to democratic participation as provided under the United Nations Declaration of Human Rights of 1948. Article 21 of the United Nations Declaration on Human Rights recognizes the concept of public participation, and Article 25 of the International Covenant on Civil and Political rights provides for every citizen's right to take part in the conduct of public affairs.

Article 13(1) of the African Charter on Human and People's Rights also provides for public participation. The content of public participation has been expanded and developed to include other rights like equality, freedom of speech and of association. Participation of the people in the conduct of public affairs must be genuine and effective. Effective public participation implies the involvement of the public and other stakeholders at all stages of the constitution making process, including in the selection of members of the constitutional review commission or technical committee.

The importance of involving as many stakeholders as possible is intended to make sure that the constitution reflects common interests of the people, not interests of a few. Constituencies or group interests that are consulted are expected to advance the interest of the general public not their own.

Public participation on its own may not necessarily lead to the writing of a democratic constitution. Public participation must be supported by certain mechanisms and strategies in order for such participation to result in the creation of a democratic constitution. These mechanisms include putting in place key transitional mechanisms that are aimed at opening up democratic space for political participation, before inviting the public to participate in the constitution making process, developing legitimate and democratic constitutional principles and using such principles to guide public participation towards the writing of a democratic constitution and using an independent tribunal to certify the final draft constitution prior to the national referendum.

It is regrettable that in many countries constitutional making processes have failed to involve the people and that instead the people have been systematically manipulated to endorse the interests of the elites.

There are many theories that inform constitution making processes. For our purposes two theories seem relevant. These are: the elitist and democratic theory. The elite theory holds that a representative democracy is not really based on the will of the people, but that there is a relatively small, cohesive elite class that makes almost all the important decisions for the nation.

Elite theorists essentially argue that a privileged few should rule in the name of the people, with a controlled amount of input from citizens. This theory seems to mistrust the people as a source of power, as the people may lack certain information or knowledge in crafting a constitution that may be required. At its worst, this theory suggests that the majority may, in certain circumstances, adopt positions that do not accord with an inclusive democratic society; and may adopt positions that oppress the minority.

Democratic theory on the other hand posits that the people should determine who governs them and under what kind of a constitution. It requires a high level of participation in constitution making, and is based on a high degree of confidence in the judgment of ordinary people.

It must be conceded that constitutional making is not a neutral process and therefore partisan forces are part of the process. The contestation between different groups in society as may be represented by political parties and other groups may result in a constitution that reflects only the interest of one group, and not the entire society. It is therefore important that everything possible should be done to ensure that a constitution reflects the aspirations of the entire society.

Experience demonstrates that effective and extensive public participation in constitution making process contributes significantly to social cohesion and national unity. Enduring constitutions cannot be imposed from above. They must reflect an agreement within the population about how to be governed. Thorough civic education, a consultative constitution making process can help address the underlying causes of poor governance and ensure that a new constitution reflects the aspirations of the people. Constitution making may also be educative in nature and an exercise in democratic empowerment in that people get to learn about what a constitution is and its importance.

A transparent and fair process should allow people to contribute their thoughts on what the constitution should provide without inhibition or undue obstruction.

CHAPTER FOUR

THE PROCESS – THE RIGHT TO PARTICIPATE

As indicated earlier the right of the people to participate in the conduct of national affairs is widely recognised by both international and regional legal instruments. In effect the right to participate in national affairs allows people to determine their destiny; in particular, how they wish to be ruled. It encourages active citizenship.

The right to participate must be effective. Effective public participation implies the involvement of the public at all stages of the constitution making process, including in the selection of members of the constitutional review commission, if that is the preferred path. The process of constitution making can only claim legitimacy and credibility if the people have been meaningfully involved in each stage of the process.

Quite often, the public is not informed about the ground rules of the process and the underlying principles, including key individual players such as the members of the constitutional review commission and experts. It is desirable that membership of the review commission should be inclusive. It is ideal that such a process must be led by a judge or a person who has held high judicial office. It is also important that the people should decide whether the process should be carried out by a general convention gathering, target groups or visiting each constituency in order to get their views on the process and content. Effective participation also implies that each community, including minorities and the disadvantaged, should be consulted. The process of consultation should leave no one behind.

The consultation process should be transparent and fair. South Africa is often cited as an example of a country that embraced thorough consultation of its people. The process of consultation included organized formations outside parliament and individual citizens. It is because of the transparent and inclusive nature of the process that was undertaken that at the end of it all the people felt the constitution belongs to them as a nation and not to certain individuals or groups.

Where it is considered necessary to use both local and international experts care must be taken that they do not assume the role of the people. An example of a constitution making process that was criticized for being dominated by local and international experts is Malawi. It was suggested that as a result of the domination of the experts the constitution did not reflect the wishes of the people but those of experts and perhaps donors.

Ideally the process must be adequately budgeted for and be funded from state funds but if for whatever reason the assistance of the donors is considered necessary care should be taken that they should not, in effect, dictate what is finally included in the constitution.

The constitutional making process should attempt to reach as many people as possible, including civil society organizations. Members of the civil society, both registered and unregistered, should be allowed to present their views both on the content and the process of constitution making.

The pre-1994 constitutional negotiations in South Africa demonstrated the important role of civil society in constitution making. All organized formations such as trade unions, lawyers' associations, gender groups and other civil society organisations made submissions that enhanced the constitution making process.

In South Africa experience shows that civil society organisations were successful when they worked together on issues, especially lobbying for a comprehensive bill of rights in the constitution. Targeting youth and religious groups is also a good idea as these groups usually constitute a significant portion of the broader populace.

The participation of marginalized groups is particularly important owing to their vulnerability. They, more than any other group, need the constitution. They need to be heard. Constitution making is also an opportunity to address gender inequality and other problems associated with marginalization and exclusion.

In South Africa, women played an important role in the constitution making process and were able to bring shared experiences and perspectives across party lines. More significantly, women were able to act in a united way in respect of gender-related issues like treatment of rural women under customary law.

Another country in which women contributed positively to the constitution making process is Rwanda. In Rwanda, women organisations organised consultative forums aimed at encouraging women to participate in the constitution making process.

The question as to who controls the agenda of the constitution making process can be a contentious issue. It is important that the people should be involved in determining the agenda of the constitution making process, including the pre, during and post phases of the drafting of the constitution.

In both South Africa and Rwanda, the elites framed the campaigns and provided personnel to the constitution making process, but gave room for the public to effectively participate in the process by receiving submissions and visiting the rural communities.

A constitutional making process needs workshops, seminars, public meetings and people that are trained and knowledgeable about the process and the constitutional issues involved. Resources permitting establishing outreach, local offices to provide information and explain the process on what a constitution is all about is an idea worth pursuing.

The credibility of the body entrusted with reviewing the constitution is equally important. It is critical that constitutional review commission or technical committees appointed to carry out the review process must enjoy a sense of credibility in the process. They must be impartial and independent. The members must be people of integrity. The credibility and competence of commissioners and experts has an impact on the outcome of the process. If the public do not perceive the commissioners to be independent, the end product would not be legitimate and they would be no sense of ownership by the people. The commissioners should not represent the interests of any political player or sectoral interests.

It has been suggested that the political leadership needs to be an honest broker throughout the whole process with the spirit of nation building. History has taught that society will not attribute legitimacy to the constitution if the leadership is seen to be corrupt or having mala fides. Political will remains one of the fundamental and underlying foundations of achieving a legitimate constitutional order.

Where there is a political will, the road map that includes time lines is always very clear. In constitution making, the time allocated for each stage and phase matters a lot. This ensures a smooth process, whose end product can be delivered in time and within budget. A constitutional review process that is done haphazardly, may never be concluded, leading to wastage of time and resources. The time that is allocated depends on the circumstances of each country.

The South African constitution making process took six years owing to the history of apartheid and the prolonged dialogue between the stake holders. The Zimbabwean constitutional process that led to the 2013 constitution took around four (4) years. The Nigerian coordinating committee was given two months and this was criticised as far inadequate. If the time allocated to a commission charged with constitution making is insufficient, it will have an adverse impact on the outcome of the process. The ultimate product may be defective and unsatisfactory. It is therefore critical to allocate sufficient time to each stage of constitution making process so that everything proceeds as smoothly as possible.

The constitution making process usually ends with the people deciding through a referendum. In the referendum, people may be asked to signal their approval of certain proposals. It is important that before the referendum is conducted, the people be educated about the referendum process and how it is conducted. The people should be aware of what they are approving and disapproving through a referendum. The choice of the terminology of what to vote for in a referendum is as important as the contents of the referendum. The referendum organizing body, ideally, the Independent Electoral Commission, should determine what people are voting for.

The process must be clearly mapped out. This includes the following aspects:

- *Determining, developing and setting up of the steering body of the constitutional reform-process;*
- *Designing the methodology and terms of reference*
- *Setting out the timeframes.*

In South Africa for instance, after the constitutional assembly was constituted, it had two years from the date of its first sitting to adopt a final constitution.

The road map to a legitimate constitution should include the following steps:

- **Stakeholder conference(s)** – these would be forums to get buy-in and input from all sectors and from citizens. Several of these can be organized at various stages of the process. The Zimbabwean process conducted two such conferences.

- **Designing broad principles that will inform the new constitution** – this includes setting up the constitutional principles through a broad consultative and participatory process. The stakeholder conferences, or whatever form of engagement may be preferred, would be central in shaping the foundational principles on whose basis the constitution-making process would unfold. Parliament may also be actively involved in this process, and/or any special body that would have been devised to lead the constitution reform process.

- *Public consultations*

- *Drafting*

- *Debate and discussion*

- *Finalization of draft*

- *Referendum or Certification* - A referendum is the ultimate seal of legitimacy and ownership. After a draft is developed, the draft may be put to a referendum, so that the people can express their wish on the social contract.

Zimbabwe and Kenya subjected their constitutions to referenda. With a referendum, the final draft is gazetted, and a campaign period follows, leading to the actual YES or NO vote. An alternative to a referendum is parliamentary adoption. However, this option has challenges in that the people may not feel ownership of the document, given that parliamentary democracy entails representation and therefore indirect participation. This may affect legitimacy. Yet another alternative is certification of the constitution. Constitutional certification is the idea that the draft constitution must be reviewed against the set constitutional principles and be certified by an impartial tribunal before being submitted for adoption through a popular referendum or a vote by the constituent assembly.

Certification involves examining the draft constitution to check if it complies with and fully gives effect to the agreed constitutional principles. This requires a totally independent and impartial body. Political actors that are engaged in constitutional negotiations must ensure that an impartial tribunal is created even where it means creating a totally new structure all together.

South Africa provides an excellent example, where the newly-established constitutional court was to be the certifying body. On the first certification attempt, the constitution was referred back to the constitutional assembly for want of compliance with certain constitutional principles, then came the second attempt, and the constitution was certified. One may also consider a combination of certification, and then subjecting the draft constitution to a referendum. What must be said is that each approach has its pros and cons, and the most ideal for the purposes and conditions of Botswana must be chosen, or a combination of the approaches.

The constitution-making process must have a start and an end. A time-line and work plan must be clearly devised to guide each and every stage of the process. The timelines must be realistic and practical, and the funding allocated to the process must take into account these timelines. The funding must be adequate. The timelines are a check mechanism to ensure finality to the process, and to ensure that work is done efficiently and effectively. The timelines must be made public, and must be adhered to.

In Zimbabwe, the COPAC-led process fell behind schedule with almost 3 years, owing to the hiccups that met the process. Such a situation ought to be avoided as it then comes with costs, but also possible cutting corners and eventually too imperfect a product.

In conclusion it cannot be over emphasized that constitution making should satisfy certain requirements such as genuine participation of the people. The people should be able to understand the importance of the constitution and should have knowledge of both the process and the content. The preceding chapters offer the necessary background and context of the constitutional review process that may take place in Botswana.

CHAPTER FIVE

WHY A NEW CONSTITUTION IS NOW AN IMPERATIVE FOR BOTSWANA?

Botswana's constitution is old and time barred. It must be fundamentally improved if it is to remain relevant to the aspirations of the people. Piecemeal amendments are not desirable if the country has its eyes set on positioning itself as a continental leader in democracy, human rights and the rule of law as it ought to be, and minimize the risk of the people disowning it as no longer relevant to their lives. The need to improve the Batswana constitution so that it may meet the demands of contemporary society is self-evident. It is about entrenching democracy and strengthening the institutions that support democracy.

Botswana's independence constitution was a product of negotiations between the colonial rulers and the nationalist leaders. It marked a symbolic end of colonialism and the ushering in of a republican state. At its minimalist conceptualization, republicanism is an ideological commitment to liberty and a rejection of hereditary rulers at the helm of the state.

The nationalist leaders who fought or agitated for independence from colonial rule were keen on self-determination and human rights. Constitutions became both symbols of statehood and of social compact. It was important both for symbolic and practical purposes that new states developed new constitutions that can live up to the promise the national leaders made to their people. The tragic story of Africa though is that soon after independence, a number of countries that had promised their people good governance, democracy and the rule of law became dictatorial and suppressed human rights.

Botswana's constitution is a classic post-colonial document that only entrenches civil and political rights. It is on the main modelled along the European Convention on Human Rights of 1950; that came into effect on the 3rd of September, 1953. As every historian and constitutionalist well knows, the country's constitution was not a product of any deliberation by the people. Owing to the wholesome changes required, a whole new constitution altogether is needed, as opposed to piecemeal changes ushered in by means of constitutional amendments with the framework remaining that of the old.

The current constitution had a transitional purpose, which it served well. However, Botswana today chases a different purpose. The nation has moved on since the post-independence transitional phase. Transition in the present now takes a different outlook: it is now about deepening democracy, consolidating democratic governance, and building a prosperous society. That calls for a renewed social contract that captures the fundamentals of the day. Exigencies of the day at independence meant that the constitution had to be a political document concerned with transition to majoritarian rule. Exigencies of today however now dictate different priorities. One of these priorities is equal access to economic opportunities.

The Botswana experience is by no means isolated. It is a typical trajectory of the post-independence African states. Over 52 years into independence, Botswana is a late bloomer at constitutional reform, from an independence transitional constitution to an elaborate broad-based social contract created with the nation's vision and wishes beyond colonial political settlements.

Hessebon in his article titled "The Fourth Constitution-Making Wave of Africa…" (2014) 28(2) *Temple Int'l & Comp. L.J.* 185 argues that the current efforts at constitutional reform in Africa are widespread and constitute what he terms "the fourth wave of constitution-making in Africa". He identifies as causes, among others, first the need to reduce the power of the executive to prevent abuse of incumbency; and second, the need to devolve government and foster constitutional decentralization to avoid politicized ethnicity. Specifically, the 2010 Kenyan constitution is identified as the most emblematic of the newest batch of African constitutions. Hessebon also references the constitutions of other

African countries, such as Nigeria, Ethiopia, Ghana, and South Africa.

Pertinent to Botswana is that these drivers towards constitutional reform in other countries do not spare Botswana. This is for various reasons, the significant of which are highlighted hereunder:

(i) ***Batswana were not directly involved in designing and adopting the current constitution***

As a basic principle, a law must serve the needs of its subjects. This means the lived realities of the subjects must form the very basis of the law and its content. This rings true of constitutions as well, and Botswana is no exception. What this means is that the people who are to be subject to a constitution must partake in the making of that constitution.

The legitimacy of the constitution derives from it being a product of the people. As indicated earlier contemporary constitution making or reforms demand that the process be given as much importance as the content of the constitution.

(ii) ***The need to align the constitution to progressive international legal norms and standards***

Botswana now belongs to the family of nations. A new constitution affords Botswana the opportunity to domesticate its international law commitments through the supreme law. This international law constitutes norms and standards that members of the civilized world have rationalized and adopted as worthy of observance, protection and enforcement.

(iii) *Urgency of achieving greater freedoms for Batswana*

Greater freedoms are not just about liberties. Rather, it is about unleashing human potential, and ensuring that Batswana operate at their optimum potential. Human rights are empowering. They unlock independence, determination, ambition, willpower, industriousness, ingenuity, innovation and creativity in the people. These are indispensable ingredients for development of any kind. These ideals are not just mere rhetoric, but are ingredients to the socio-economic and political development of the country.

(iv) *Botswana is on a journey of economy development*

Good governance is a pre-requisite for economic development. Good governance in turn is enabled and facilitated by a sound constitution, which amongst other things, underpins the rule of law and property rights and administrative justice.

(v) *Deepening democracy - Botswana is now a democracy powerhouse in Africa*

For Botswana to continue to build its brand as a leading democracy in Africa (a brand which has attracted to it goodwill, investments and respect) it must join the progressive nations of the world with 21st century, purpose-built and progressive constitution.

CHAPTER SIX

AN OVERVIEW OF BROAD CONSTITUTIONAL PRINCIPLES THAT MUST GUIDE THE CONSTITUTIONAL MAKING PROCESS

For a constitutional-reform process to assume direction and substance, a set of principles should be negotiated and devised. These will guide and determine the process. They will determine the broad framework and thinking within which the constitution must be made.

Basically, constitutional principles are a set of minimum standards that the final constitution must fulfill and seek to advance. A set of constitutional principles creates a vision of a constitution to be produced out of the constitution making process. This vision will guide the public to identify the nature of the views they must submit during the public consultation phase. They will also guide the drafting process in the sense that the drafters can rely on the constitutional principles to interpret the views submitted by the public. In that way, constitutional principles assist to stimulate and guide constitutional imagination and drafting during the constitution making process.

Constitutional principles must never be imposed upon the people. Thus, when developing constitutional principles, the government must ensure that all the key social, religious, civil society and political groups are involved in order to secure the legitimacy of the resultant constitutional principles. If the constitutional principles are legitimate, then it is possible and appropriate to subject the entire constitution making process and public views to those principles. It is possible to develop consensus on a set of constitutional principles through an inclusive process of continuous deliberation and negotiations.

In South Africa thirty-four constitutional principles were agreed upon, to which the final constitution would have to adhere to. It had been agreed that the constitutional court would adjudicate the adherence to these principles by certifying the constitution, once it had been passed by the constitutional assembly.

A selection of principles includes: supremacy of the constitution; a commitment to the rule of law; keeping executive powers in check; judicial independence; transparent and accountable government; protection of human rights; equality of all before the law; decentralizing or devolving power; an independent central bank, regulating political parties; establishing an inclusive electoral system; separation of powers between the executive, legislature and the judiciary; the judiciary must be appropriately qualified; the institution and role of traditional leadership; entrenchment of the constitution against amendments; and the limitation of rights. The above list should not be regarded as exhaustive but merely as examples of principles that may be agreed upon.

In Zimbabwe, the Global Political Agreement (GPA) contained constitutional principles. These formed the basis of a set of Talking Points, which Talking Points were the discussion points in the public consultations. Through article VI of the GPA, the parties undertook to conduct a "people-driven" constitution making process that would produce a constitution that "deepens democratic values and principles".

Essentially the parties to the GPA committed themselves to undertake a constitution making process that is based on extensive public participation and that produces a democratic constitution. Article VI of the GPA outlined the key stages which the intended constitution making process would involve in order to ensure that the process was based on public participation.

As Justice Alfred Mavedzenge argued in his thesis of 2014, one of the reasons why public participation in a constitution making process may not result in the writing of a democratic constitution is the absence of a framework or constitutional vision that guides the people towards writing a democratic constitution. Without this, it cannot be assumed that a democratic constitution will emerge out of a participatory constitution making process. As such there must be a framework that is put in place to deliberately guide the public participatory process towards achieving the desired democratic constitution.

Experiences from contemporary participatory constitution making exercises like that of South Africa and Namibia have demonstrated that it is possible to produce legitimate, democratic constitutional principles through a participatory process.

In Zimbabwe, although the political leaders agreed to a set of constitutional principles, the process of developing those principles was exclusive and ad hoc. There were no consultations beyond the parties in the Government of National Unity, and the decision to develop those constitutional principles appeared to have been made as an afterthought, because the official programme of the constitution making process did not include developing a set of constitutional principles.

The principle of public participation is particularly important. Public participation is the fulcrum of the constitution-making process. The participation of the public is one of the key motivations for instigating a new constitution-making process. It is important that there must be real public participation with real impact and influence, not merely cosmetic public consultation to create or paint a picture of broad-participation. What this means is that the process:

- must be genuinely participatory;
- must not be rushed;

- must accord all the opportunity to participate;

- must have various methods and platforms of participation; and

- must be accompanied by the necessary empowerment for people to have informed and meaningful participation in the process.

In South Africa the public was encouraged to make submissions regarding the contents of the final constitution. A vast number of submissions were received, but it is highly unlikely that many of them were even perused, let alone considered. Whatever the original intention, the exercise eventually became a means of giving the constitution legitimacy by encouraging the "buy-in" of the public, rather than a means of gathering opinion or comment on any of the specific provisions.

The new constitution must seek to deepen and entrench democracy. Botswana has in the past decades reaped benefits from democratic practice, and it is fair to say democracy as a system of government has worked well. It only makes sense to deepen and consolidate that democracy. The traditional four (4) forms of democracy must be reflected in the new constitution: representative, participatory, direct and constitutional:

- Representative democracy – participation in governance through elected representatives and political parties;

- Participatory democracy – opportunities to participate in decision making that is/on issues that are affecting them;

- Direct democracy - major political decision taken by people themselves; and

- Constitutional democracy - people's representatives in parliament, the legislature and the judiciary are bound by the norms and values of the constitution.

The line consistent with the trajectory Botswana is moving currently, is liberal and republican democracy. It is a democracy associated with pluralism – respect for diversity, no forced assimilation, multiparty political systems, and has tenets opposed to dictatorship, oligarchy, plutocracy, kleptocracy and totalitarianism.

In drafting a new constitution, Botswana must also bear in mind the standards and principles set out in the African Charter on Democracy, Elections, and Governance (ACDEG). Article 10 of ACDEG is instructive and provides:

"1. State Parties shall entrench the principle of the supremacy of the constitution in the political organization of the State.

2. State Parties shall ensure that the process of amendment or revision of their constitution reposes on national consensus, obtained if need be, through referendum."

Modern constitutional making should also be constrained and shaped by the international standards to which all countries have assented, as captured by the Universal Declaration of Human Rights and other relevant regional instruments such as the African Charter on Human and Peoples' Rights.

CHAPTER SEVEN

REFLECTING ON POSSIBLE SUBSTANTIVE PROVISIONS OF THE NEW CONSTITUTION

It is important that a constitution should clearly outline, at the very beginning, the founding provisions for the state. Ideally, the introductory chapter should make it clear that the constitution is the supreme law of the land and that any law, practice, custom or conduct inconsistent with it is invalid to the extent of the inconsistency. This is important so as to make it plain to any person that the constitution is superior to any law and guard against possible undermining of the constitution.

Our constitution does not make this point categorically clear. The conclusion that the constitution is superior is implied from its character and totality of its provisions. Reading the constitution as a whole our courts have held that the constitution is the supreme law.

The introductory chapter may also state the founding values and principles including "the rule of law," "fundamental human rights and freedoms," "observance of the principle of separation of powers," "human dignity" "democracy" and other values that capture the essence of constitutionalism and the rule of law.

It may also be a good idea for the constitution to oblige the state to "promote public awareness of the constitution," through translating it into all languages spoken in the country, teaching it in schools, including it in curricula for all public employees, and encouraging everyone to disseminate it as widely as possible. It is important that the constitution should promote the belief that, unless people know, cherish, uphold, and demand respect for their constitution, it will remain a glorified piece of paper.

A Comprehensive and Transformative Bill of Rights

The new constitution should provide for a wide, comprehensive and fully justiciable bill of rights, which includes civil and political rights, as well as economic, social and cultural rights.

Additionally, the new constitution may include a chapter on national objectives, which sets out a list of obligations, to guide the state in formulating and implementing laws and policy decisions. These obligations, may or may not create corresponding and individually justiciable rights enforceable in a court of law. The nation would have to debate which option they prefer.

In some jurisdictions that have a chapter on national objectives, courts are required to take them into account when interpreting the bill of rights. This can facilitate a more expansive interpretation of rights. Some constitutions like the Zimbabwean 2013 constitution do not explicitly rule out the justiciability of the national objectives. Other country's constitutions with similar chapters include clauses that explicitly negate courts' jurisdiction over the enforcement of the rights and obligations contained therein.

It may be important for the new constitution to impose duties on both the state and private persons, including juristic persons, with regard to the bill of rights, by making it clear that both the state and every person, including juristic persons, must respect, protect, promote and fulfil the rights and freedoms set out in the bill of rights.

Making private power accountable to the law in so far as human rights are concerned makes sense in the contemporary era, where multinational corporations and other big businesses, may in some circumstances, hold as much power as states or even more. In my mind, it may make sense that mechanisms be put in place to hold juristic persons to account, not only for human rights abuses, but also to actively work to protect, promote and fulfil human rights.

The inclusion of justiciable economic, social and cultural rights in the bill of rights would represent a significant step forward as well. As with many other countries, our constitution did not protect such rights. These socio – economic rights should be comprehensive and possibly include rights to: education; healthcare; food and water; clean environment and other environmental rights; fair labor practices; freedom of profession, trade or occupation; language and culture; and marriage. There could also be socio-economic rights protected for specific groups, such as a right to: nutrition and shelter for children; welfare for the elderly over the age of 65 years, pregnant women and special educational and medical needs for persons with disabilities.

The nation would have to debate what approach the courts should take in interpreting socio – economic rights. There are basically two approaches: the "reasonableness approach" or the "minimum core approach". Basically, the reasonableness approach permits the courts to incrementally enforce socio – economic rights based usually on the evidence that the state is in a position to honour those rights, given the resources available. This is the approach that has largely been favoured by the South African Constitutional Court. Some people do not consider this approach sufficiently protective of rights.

In academic literature disagreements remain about the content, scope and even utility of the "minimum core" concept. At the very minimum, it could be said that this approach seeks to set a quantitative, and qualitative floor of minimum requirements that must be met with respect to each of the economic and cultural rights that must be realised by the state, as a matter of top priority.

We must debate the question whether we want our courts to adopt the "reasonableness approach" developed by the South African constitutional court, or the "minimum core approach" espoused by the United Nations Committee on Economic, Social and Cultural Rights. Other courts, such as the Colombian constitutional court, have adopted the "minimum core approach," while still others, such as the Indian supreme court, have taken, what may be called the middle path.

It may also be necessary to revisit some constitutional provisions that have been considered controversial or not sufficiently protective of human rights. I discuss a few such examples below. The list is by no means exhaustive.

The Right to Life and the Death Penalty

The death penalty in Botswana is constitutional. It is up to the nation to revisit how they wish to reframe the right to life in the new constitution, if so inclined. One option is to simply entrench the right to life and say nothing about the death penalty and leave it to the courts to interpret what the right to life entails. This will leave the question whether the death penalty violates the right to life or not, to the courts to interpret as happened in South Africa.

It should not be taken for granted that a consultative process will necessarily lead to a more democratic or pro rights constitution in all respects. In fact with respect to the death penalty the opposite may be true. The general populace may be more conservatively inclined and insist on retaining the death penalty, (which is their prerogative). This view of the populace may run counter to prevailing international law that considers the death penalty a violation of the right to life.

Equality and Non-discrimination

The rights to equality and freedom from discrimination are enshrined in section three (3) and (15) of our constitution, respectively. We may wish to strengthen section three (3) consistent with experience and our reality. In societies such as ours with a history of discrimination, particularly on the grounds of gender, health status and sexual orientation, this would be a positive development.

Section 15 of the constitution includes a list of grounds on which discrimination is prohibited. This list does not explicitly include sexual orientation, health and marital status among other permissible grounds. We have the option to increase the list of prohibited grounds consistent with international law or make it clear in the constitution that this list is open and subject to development by the courts based on the "rationality" test.

The new constitution may also include women's rights such as: sexual reproductive and health rights; the right to be protected from all forms of discrimination, abuse, injustice, violence, harmful traditions. It should also offer women protection of employment during pregnancy, after delivery, and to own property of all kinds. The constitution may also provide that the clause prohibiting non-discrimination should not prevent government from taking affirmative action measures to redress past injustices.

There must also be provisions to protect special rights of children, youth, the elderly, persons with disabilities, minority groups and other vulnerable persons.

Mechanisms for Government Accountability and Transparency

The need to limit and control the powers of government, especially, the executive, has philosophical roots in the notions of democracy which emphasize that government has no right to govern, save with the consent of the governed.

Botswana is a Republic. This means the country has shifted away from traditional mode of governance. In traditional African societies power is perceived as personal, mystical and pervasive. The chief is a ruler who usually rules for life; often serving as judge, legislator, priest, rainmaker and more. Botswana moved away from feudal mode of governance about 53 years ago. Botswana must modernize. During the feudal era mechanisms for accountability where not always clear as a lot of power was centered on the ruler.

The constitution may oblige the state to adopt policies and legislation to develop accountability, transparency, personal integrity and financial probity in every government agency or institution. Additionally, the constitution may oblige all agencies and institutions of government—especially independent commissions, to be given adequate resources and facilities to carry out their functions diligently, the rationale being that if they have sufficient resources, they may be less prone to corruption.

The constitution should ideally entrust parliament with the responsibility of an oversight role in holding the executive accountable, by requiring, among others, that the president, vice president, minister and deputy minister unless lawfully excused, should attend parliament and parliamentary committees in order to answer questions concerning matters for which he or she is collectively or individually responsible. Given the problem of absenteeism in parliament this would place a constitutional obligation on every member of the executive branch to answer questions before parliament.

It may also be an interesting innovation to provide in the constitution that every member of parliament, executive, and public service is obliged to put the interest of the country first in any decision taken in exercise of official duty.

Alternatively, the constitution may prescribe that every exercise of public power must be justifiable. In consequence of the above provisions, it may be possible to ensure that parliamentarians should not simply toe the party line, but should represent and convey the concerns of their constituents, in order to hold government to account and to put the interest of country first. Similarly, it may be a good idea to oblige the president, at such times as may be deemed fit, to answer questions on the state of the nation from members of parliament. This would clearly be an improvement on the previous constitution, under which the president had no obligation to attend parliament at all.

Transparency may also be promoted by requiring that the leadership of the country as may be defined, which should include all constitutional office holders, should subscribe to a prescribed code of ethics administered by a commission of public officials.

The people may also wish to debate the question whether they want the president to be directly elected and or for cabinet to be drawn from outside parliament or not. The constitution may need to clearly prescribe other checks and balances mechanisms such as a motion of no confidence against the president of the day or government or prescribe circumstances under which the president may be impeached. Grounds of impeachment may include: contravention of the constitution, bribery and other serious offences, obstruction of justice, failure to obey court orders and contravention of code of conduct of the national leadership.

The constitution may also prescribe the threshold for a motion of no confidence, by prescribing that a motion of no confidence may be passed by a simple majority or two-thirds of elected members of the national assembly.

Access to Information

The bill of rights should ideally, entrench the right to access official information, by providing that every citizen or permanent resident, including juristic persons and the media, in the country, has the right of access to any information held by the state or by any institution or agency of government at every level, in so far as the information is required in the interests of public accountability. It should be possible to provide for restrictions to this right only in the interests of defence, public security or professional accountability, and to the extent that the restriction is fair, reasonable, necessary and justifiable in a democratic society based on openness, justice, human dignity, equality and freedom.

Devolution

Devolution seems an imperative of our time. It will make local councils accountable to the electorate rather than the national government. Local councils are much closer to the people and must be given sufficient autonomy and power to be responsive to the wishes and aspirations of local communities. The nation may wish to debate whether local government structures should involve traditional leadership or not.

Batswana must debate whether they would want to foster equitable development nationwide by devolving power and giving more autonomy to local government structures. The matter of distribution of power should be debated carefully. Issues of devolution of power to local governments are important as part of deepening democracy. This may result in the phenomenon of executive mayors for instance. Centralized systems are a remnant of the colonial era, where governance was predicated on power and control over development and facilitating independence.

Contemporary constitutional reform efforts in Africa have tended to put emphasis on devolution/decentralization. Previous constitutional reform waves were dominated by the view that a centralized form of authority is necessary to guarantee the unity and territorial integrity of states. In the past, regional autonomy and federalism were viewed with suspicion. Furthermore, ethno-cultural differences were ignored and given little or no constitutional recognition. With the rhetorical denunciation of tribalism, previous constitutions adopted a hostile attitude to ethnicity. However, a shift is now evident, owing to the tried and tested benefits of devolution and decentralization.

Judicial Independence

The judiciary in Botswana is required to be independent. However, nowhere does the constitution provide for the independence of the judiciary in express terms. The constitution should clearly provide that the courts are independent and subject only to the constitution and the law, and must apply the law impartially, expeditiously and without fear, favour or prejudice. The process for the appointment of judges and the involvement of politicians should be debated. It may be a good idea to remove the appointment process from the clutches of politicians.

Alternatively, if it is deemed necessary for politicians to play a part in the appointment of judges, then the constitution may prescribe a minimum role for them.

Among judicial reforms that must be articulated are a transparent and merit-based system of appointing judges. The appointment of judges is a crucial gatekeeper that determines who goes to the bench, holding what philosophy and doing what with it, and to whom and in what manner they are accountable. The very functioning of the courts is dependent on who sits on the bench. The trajectory must move from a situation where the president has expansive appointment powers, to a situation where the process is much more transparent and insulated from political manipulation. Public interviews of the prospective candidates would be a noble idea; which has been successfully followed in South Africa, Kenya and now recently in Zimbabwe.

It must be a requirement that appointments to the judiciary must reflect broadly the diversity and gender composition of Botswana. The judicial service commission must become much more representative, and not just be composed of executive-appointed officials, or just members of the judiciary. This is important because the extent to which the appointment of judges is free from political manipulation is largely reliant on the independence of the judicial service commission.

The constitution may wish to carefully delineate the power of the judiciary in the broader constitutional scheme and decide what checks and balances they want to infuse into the constitution. The new constitution may also answer the question whether it is necessary to restructure the court system, have a unitary judiciary headed by the chief justice or maintain the current set up where the court of appeal is headed by the judge president.

A transformative bill of rights requires an intellectually transformed judiciary. History teaches that an intellectually untransformed judiciary is the gravest threat to a transformative ambition of the constitution, as the debate in Kenya clearly demonstrates. Recently, on the 24th of May, 2019, the High Court of Kenya, notwithstanding a constitution regarded as progressive, declined to declare criminalization of gay sex unconstitutional. This decision drew strong condemnation by the United Nations and rights activists.

A second suggested reform would be to create a new apex court in the form of a constitutional court.

The benefits of a new constitutional court are that it creates a break from the past in the judiciary, allowing a new breed of legal minds to take charge of constitutional adjudication and operationalizing the new constitution. This would be a court to deal with the difficult and sensitive issues to do with governance and constitutional interpretation and enforcement.

There is, in my mind, an urgent need for a constitutional court to lead the process of judicial transformation. The goal is to achieve a transformed judiciary beholden to nothing but the constitution and the law, and to achieve transformative adjudication. This is the very same reason South Africa adopted a constitutional court in the 1993 interim constitution at the turn of democracy.

The South African constitutional court was to be a clean break from the past, so that new untainted judges who were not part of the apartheid court system could lead the process of constitutional interpretation and enforcement; making decisions which would bind all the lower courts. The new constitutional court was to serve the purpose of specialized constitutional interpretation and litigation, and lend legitimacy to the process. The South African approach was a world-renowned success.

Separation of Powers

Nowhere does our constitution provide, in explicit terms for separation of powers. The doctrine of separation of powers consists of several principles, including: institutional division of state governance; independence of each branch from control by another; financial independence; oversight; and checks and balances. Currently, the executive remains the most powerful branch of government. The new constitution may have to provide for some checks on executive power, and oversight mechanisms to hold each of the three branches accountable. It may also be time to debate whether the vice president should be elected by the people or keep the current position where he is effectively chosen by the president.

The new constitution must clearly articulate the separation of powers and this must be reflected in the institutional structuring, as well as the powers given to each arm and institutions of government. An example of specificity in separation of powers when it comes to institutions is that the constitution may consider separating the Attorney-General and prosecutorial work completely, and devising a new prosecuting authority with its own head to independently conduct public prosecutions, without the need to consult the Attorney General in so – called cases of national importance.

Batswana must debate whether they want a stronger executive and an independent parliament. They must also debate whether they want to give the president a blank cheque in appointing and dismissing ministers and other senior government officials. It may also be time to revisit the nature, name and composition of the *Ntlo –Ya Dikgosi* (House of Chiefs) and its functions.

The people may wish to debate what other oversight institutions they want to establish. Other countries have, for instance, the Auditor General, Independent Electoral Commissions, Public Accounts Committee, Human Rights Commissions as constitutional creations. The other matter relates to the question whether the people also want a constitutional body overseeing the media and police or security agencies' work?

I discuss the above institutions and their possible functions below.

With respect to oversight institutions, the constitution may define their structure, composition and functions in a manner that ensures that there is no undue interference with their operations. An additional constitutional provision to the effect that any legislation, measures or conduct which undermines the essential purpose of accountability and transparency that the institution is designed to achieve shall be deemed to be invalid, may be helpful.

Batswana must debate whether they want separation of mandates between the cabinet and parliament and say whether they are happy with double loyalties to both institutions; whether they want a merit based system of appointment of the civil service including the head of the civil service. They must debate the electoral system they desire. A more inclusive formulation promotes stability and is in keeping with the modern trend. The choice of an electoral system depends on where we come from as a nation, and where we want to go. The constitution may also prescribe and or regulate public funding of political parties and party funding generally.

It is imperative, however, that a constitution of the 21st century must entrench the right to free and fair elections. It is high time that the constitution must recognize the basic rights and duties of political parties; which are currently not mentioned in the constitution. The constitution may also provide how political parties are registered and the minimum requirements to be met in order to be registered. The advantage of constitutionalizing their status is that they will come under public scrutiny at all times, not just during elections.

Provision of Independent Constitutional Institutions

The independent commissions supporting democracy may, among other things, include, the Human Rights Commission, the Gender Commission, the Media Commission, the Independent Police Complaints Commission and the Office of the Public Protector. These commissions should be independent and not subject to the direction or control of anyone.

Members of the commissions may be appointed by the president after consulting the national assembly or with the concurrence of the national assembly and may be removed using the same procedures that are used to remove judges. It may also be a good innovation that all heads of independent commissions must be certified as qualified, fit and proper by a panel of judges sitting in an open court.

The above institutions serve the role of ombudsman and public protectors, and ensure institutional efficiency and compliance with the law, transparency and accountability of officials and institutions, and greater observance and protection of human rights in the country. They are clothed with investigative powers, and the powers to recommend remedial action to the government and its arms. These institutions are independent and operate only subject to the law and to the constitution alone, and are accountable to parliament. They receive funding directly from the consolidated revenue fund through the parliament budget vote.

Below I discuss some of the common institutions established to support democracy.

Human Rights Commission

The constitution may also establish a human rights commission to specifically protect human rights. Members of the human rights commission may be appointed by the president in consultation with the judicial service commission and or by the president after consulting the national assembly or with the occurrence of the national assembly.

It is important that members must be selected for their integrity and their knowledge and understanding of, and experience in, the promotion of human rights. A prohibition that commissioners may not be members of political parties may be a good idea. It may be a requirement that upon appointment a member of the human rights commission should resign from any membership of a political party they may hold.

Auditor-General

Our constitution provides for an auditor-general whose functions, amongst other things, include, to audit the accounts, financial systems and financial management of all departments, institutions and agencies of government, and other related functions. The auditor general is appointed by the president without the involvement of parliament. It may be a good innovation to involve parliament in his or her appointment in such a way as to ring fence his/her independence. In practice, and on average, over the years, the auditor-generals, have built a reputation for independence and exposing waste and corruption in government departments.

Office of the Public Protector

Botswana has the office of the public protector. Its mandate is to attend to issues of maladministration. It is called the office of the ombudsman. It is established by an act of parliament and not the constitution. Its independence is a matter of debate. It may be wise to migrate the office to the constitution and ring fence its independence.

Gender Commission

The constitution may establish a gender commission whose mandate would be to address systemic barriers to gender equality, and to oversee the country's adherence to regional and international gender equality instruments and agreements. As an entity set up to support democracy, it must be independent and its members appointed in the same way as members of the human rights commission are appointed.

International Law and the Protection of Fundamental Rights

Our constitution does not make reference to international law. Most constitutions either make international law part of the domestic legal system or allow the courts to have regard to international law when interpreting domestic law under certain circumstances. For instance, section 362(1) of the constitution of Zimbabwe states that customary international law is part of the law in Zimbabwe, unless it is inconsistent with the constitution or an Act of Parliament.

Section 327 of the Zimbabwe constitution states that an international treaty which has been concluded or executed by the president is not binding on Zimbabwe until it has been approved by parliament; and does not form part of the law of Zimbabwe unless it is incorporated through an Act of Parliament. Botswana may chose its own path or place its own innovative limitations on the use of international law.

Given that a number of International treaties Botswana ratifies often do not get domesticated or translated into domestic legislation, it may be a good idea to place an obligation on the state to ensure that all international conventions, treaties and agreements to which Botswana is a party are incorporated into domestic law. This would mean that the state would be constitutionally required to domesticate International treaties it ratifies. Alternatively, the constitution may oblige the courts to take into account international law when interpreting provisions of the bill of rights, and that as far as possible, courts should interpret the rights enshrined in the constitution in a manner consistent with international human rights norms.

CHAPTER EIGHT

CONCLUSION

In the Botswana context, constitution-making is about improving the constitution that is clearly time barred; it is about strengthening the institutions that support democracy. The future of Botswana is predicated on the development of constitutional arrangements that guarantee a better life for all Batswana. The time for a new constitution in Botswana has come and we should make sure that the process is thorough and engenders legitimacy, and acts as a lesson to many other countries who may want to review their constitutions.

If a new constitution is not ushered in or is otherwise not legitimate, it would only be a matter of time before a constitutional crisis impresses upon the need for one. It is better to pre-empt such and be proactive, rather than wait for the day of reckoning. That day of reckoning may come with weakening of democracy; that is a risk the country should dare not take.

In recent past, constitution making across the world has taken centre stage in the quest for democracy and the rule of law. Increasingly, focus is shifting to the importance of process in order to produce legitimate constitutions that people can proudly identify with. As demonstrated in earlier chapters, many countries that failed to set up effective and genuine dialogue mechanisms that involve civil society and other stakeholders have ended up with either failed processes or constitutions whose legitimacy is still in doubt.

There is no uniform or best method of constitution making in the world. However, there are some basic standards that most constitution making states should fulfil in order to have a constitution that enjoys legitimacy among the people.

The following factors or considerations have the potential to lead to a smooth, meaningful and productive constitution making process:

- The process of constitution making is as important as the substantive provisions of a constitution.

- The constitution making process must be participatory, people driven, transparent and fair.

- The consultation phase should include the marginalized, the disabled, women and youth from both rural and urban areas.

- The religious denominations should be consulted.

- No political formation should hijack or be allowed to manipulate the process.

- The committee of experts that may be engaged should be impartial and independent and should at all times act impartially and avoid partisan politics.

- The committee of experts should not take over the role of the people and impose their views on the constitution.

- The appointment of the constitutional review committee or technical committee should be transparent.

- There is need to educate the public and embark on an extensive campaign about the constitution making process and the possible contents of the constitution, especially the bill of rights.

- The people should be informed and educated before they go for/to the constitutional referendum.

In order to create a conducive environment for free political participation, and for a smooth transition from the old to the new constitution, some transitional mechanisms may be put in place, as may be necessary. Transitional mechanisms are legal and political reforms that are often introduced to facilitate the transition from the old to the new constitutional order.

The transitional mechanisms may be more appropriate for deeply divided polities or countries emerging out of conflict; they serve the purpose of creating democratic space for free political participation. For instance, transitional mechanisms could entail the repeal and amendment of certain draconian laws that restrict the basic freedoms necessary for free political participation. The transitional mechanisms may not be necessary in Botswana except to guarantee total freedom of the people to craft a constitution of their choice.

INDEX

B

C

L

M

N

O

P

S

Saint Edward the Confessor. *See* Edward the Confessor

semi-presidential governments, 35

separation of powers, 19, 24-25, 66, 73, 85-86

socio-economic and political reality, 13

South Africa. *See* parliamentary democracies

sphere of influence, 25

Stephen, 28

supremacy of the constitution, 23, 66, 70

T

Tanzania, 9-10, 39, 41

The Africa We Want, 14

The Fourth Constitution, 61

the Great Charter of English liberties, 28

thirty-four constitutional principles, 66

three arms of government, 25

three organs of the state, 25

totalitarianism, 70

trade unions. *See* organized formations

transparent and accountable government, 66

U

undue and unjustifiable alteration, 24

United Kingdom. *See* parliamentary democracies

United Nations Declaration on Human Rights, 45

United States, 31-34

Universal Declaration of Human Rights, 71

unwritten constitution, 33

US Constitution, 32-33